DEEDS AND THEIR DAYS

Peter Fallon

DEEDS AND THEIR DAYS

after Hesiod

Gallery Books

Deeds and Their Days
is first published
simultaneously in paperback
and in a clothbound edition
on 26 October 2017.

The Gallery Press
Loughcrew
Oldcastle
County Meath
Ireland

www.gallerypress.com

ISBN 978 1 91133 721 8 *paperback*
      978 1 91133 722 5 *clothbound*

A CIP catalogue record for this book
is available from the British Library.

Deeds and Their Days receives financial assistance
from the Arts Council.

the arts council
chomhairle
ealaíon

funding
literature
artscouncil.ie

Contents

in memory of
Bairbre Dowling

Come. Come sing, O Muses
from Pieria, your songs
    are passageways to glory.
Sing to proclaim your father's
praise, Zeus, the great,
    by whose resolve the story

of a man endures in mouths   5
of many, exalted,
    or withers in oblivion.
No bother to him to proffer power,
to quash the powerful
    or to make the meek live on

while he brings down the high
and mighty. Zeus, it's true,
    who thunders from sheer
heights puts wrongs to right and —
no bother either — quells those
    who are impertinent. Hear,

Zeus, my plea, look down on me
and answer. What you decide   10
    I'll know is true.
And so I'll tell the truth
to Perses, the whole and nothing but.
    There are in fact, *two*

Strifes on earth. For Strife
is not an only child. One
        wins praise, the other blame.
They're chalk and cheese.
One's bent on discord; battles
        and a war her aim.

No man can tolerate her ways,
but her divine connections
        guarantee a share for her
of honour due. The other one's
the child of Night,
        dark Night's elder daughter.

The son of Cronos, he whose abode
is indeed a lofty mansion,
        set her with the seeds
of earth. And so she grew
to advance the lot of man. A better bet
        by far, she proceeds

to roust the indolent to industry.
He who sees another's means accrued
        through the prod
to plow and plant and puts in order
his whole house
        hungers for the same. The roughshod

rush to riches engenders grudges
in the mind of neighbours. This Strife
        does good in mortal men.
The man who fashions pots and craftsmen
who turn bowls throw envious eyes
        on the accomplishments of others. Then

one pauper vies with another,
as poet does with poet.
    Mind my words well,
Perses, and don't allow that Strife
who revels in adversities
    of those same others quell

a zeal for work or you'll
end hanging with the rabble
    in the market place.
How little they mean to him,   30
the madding crowd, who has not
    heaped his storage space

with the season's gift, the grain
of Demeter, stuff from open fields.
    Gather your plants, then relax
and observe as men begin to mill
and dissent over the assets
    in a neighbour's stacks.

Waste no time. Seize this chance,   35
the only one, for the principle
    of law — Zeus
at his most fair — to settle
our score. They split our legacy
    between us for our use

to pay off those rapacious
Powers-that-Be, fools
    on the backhand made to rule
in our dispute. You snatched
the bigger half and slinked
    away with it. Each is a fool   40

who'd not hear or heed
that one good half is better than
  any one bad whole, or learn
the worth of poor soil's pickings,
asphodel and mallow.
  Gods keep the way to earn

a living concealed from men
for if they didn't a single day's
  exertions could keep
a man for one long year,
no more to do. He'd hang his rudder up
45 above his hearth, sleep

and turn no thought to work
with teams of oxen and unflagging mules.
  Zeus burned
with rage and obscured the ways
to live once Prometheus
  outwitted him and turned

the tables on him. That's the why Zeus
devised men's woes
50 and worries. His gambit
was to conceal fire. In turn,
Prometheus, the princely son
  of Iapetus, reclaimed it

for the benefit of man from Zeus,
giver of good advice. In the tiny
  tunnel of a fennel stalk
he stole off with it unseen by him,
whom thunder thrills, which made
  the cloud collector's talk

a loud eruption. 'Son of Iapetus,   55
ace of trickery and so delighted
        with yourself and your chicanery,
the theft of fire will weigh on you
and all of men to come. The price
        you'll pay will be ubiquity

of evil, a hex attending men
which they'll cling to
        as they embrace their destinies.'
And having so pronounced   60
he laughed out loud, the father
        both of gods and mortal entities.

Then he commanded that Hephaestus
hurry to compound water and earth
        and the renowned smith
infused them, as decreed —
the face such as a goddess's,
        the form a maiden's — both allied with

a human force and voice.   65
He had Athena school her
        in the arts, such as embroidery,
and Aphrodite endow her head
with grace and with a love
        that could be

said to eat one up. Then he instructed
Hermes, the herald Argos' killer,
        to make her a right bitch
and instil in her a knavish
personality. So said Zeus,   70
        their lord, son of Cronos. Which

as he bid they did. He didn't dally,
the redoubtable and dexterous god.
      Hephaestus, though hamstrung,
then fashioned out of earth, as Zeus
ordained, the image of a modest maiden
      on whom Athena hung,

owl-eyed Athena, an outfit
of exquisite finery. Then the godly Graces
      and powerful Persuasion
bestowed on her torcs of gold
and tended to her every need,
      each fair- and fine-haired season,

and placed on her a chaplet
of spring blooms. Pallas Athena
      then decorated her with gems
and jewels, all sorts of ornaments,
and he who slaughtered Argos, Hermes —
      another of the stratagems

of Zeus, who charges Thunder —
fitted to her very being lies, cajoling
      lies, and that rogue disposition. Then
the gods' emissary installed in her
a voice and christened her Pandora
      and each denizen

of Mount Olympus agreed to give
her as a present: for struggling man
      she was a scourge.
And when the Father'd finished
his fiendish intrigue
      he dispatched a demi-urge

with the gods' gift to Epimetheus
who paid but little heed
    to the admonition
of Prometheus not to accept
an offering from Zeus, no,
    not ever, on no condition,

but to repel it for fear
some awful evil in it might
    befall mankind. He took   90
it in with open arms and then
it dawned on him. For once
    upon a time, unshook

by weight of suffering and sorrow
and the sentence of hard labour
    or those sore sicknesses
that are the harbingers of death,
the all of which put years on men
    before their time, all such stresses,

tribes had roamed the world.
This woman then removed   95
    the heavy cover from the jar and, yon
and hither, strewed its contents.
What then for men but grievous
    grief? Naught in her garrison

but Hope remained, a captive
held securely in the jar
    because, submitting to the will
of Zeus, the cloud-collector,
Pandora slammed the lid   100
    before she could escape. A fill

of misery for earth and sea,
as, like countless shades, other griefs
      patrol the universe.
There's sickness that will strike
by day and diseases that will infiltrate
      small hours like a curse

distributing their aches and pains.
Zeus, the wise one,
      stole their tongue.
There's no way to avoid his schemes.
I'll give all from the root to bloom
      if you would like to hear it sung.

But mind this well, from where
they sprang, gods and men,
      it's both one and the same.
From Time's beginning the gods who dwell
on Mount Olympus made a race of men,
      a golden race, whose second name

is Death. At that time Cronos ruled
the heavens, their lives as if
      divine, with not a single care
in mind, pain and distress
both absent thoughts. The sores of age
      left them alone, and unaware,

and their unflagging strength
allowed them to partake of lengthy
      feasts, far from harm's
way. Death like a drowsy cloud
whelmed over them, and all
      they wanted a mere arm's

105

110

115

length away. Grain-granting grounds
demanded nothing in the way
        of effort, a harvest
swelled before them. Nothing barred
to them. Theirs was good life,   120
        peace and plenty and the best

of flocks. Lights that they were
in the eyes of the Divines until
        Earth took them over and — woe betide —
they became the revenants — guardian
angels shoving injuries
        and hurts aside —

supervising cases in the courts   125
and looking out for wrongdoings
        as in a misty shroud
they stravaig throughout the land.
To dole out wealth by royal decree
        they're now allowed.

But then they made another race, those gods
on Mount Olympus, one much worse —
        not like the first in looks or mind —
and this time silver and not gold.   130
Their doting mothers coddled them
        when young and kept them behind

a century at the centre
of their houses until they stood
        on the threshold of the door
to puberty and they'd begin to fail,
bent beneath the pang of unknowing.
        What could then restrain them, poor   135

mites, from those acts of selfish pride,
one against a neighbour when
        from worship they'd abstained
and offerings at altars, the requisite
of local practices. So later, Zeus,
        Cronos' son, in rage restrained

140   them all for they refused to pay
the gods from Mount Olympus
        due respects. Earth
took them over too. Subordinate,
they live below the ground, holy humans,
        still in a state of honoured worth.

Then Zeus, the father, made another
145   race, a third, this time bronze,
        not silver, nor in any way
akin to that other, but warriors emerging
from ash groves of awful night and armed
        with spears of ash, each a devotée

of Ares, mind set on fire and fury.
Not for them ordinary food
        or fare, their hearts
were hard as stone. None could match
or near them. They were so
150   strong, with body parts

sprouting from the sturdy boles
of their physiques. Bronze was the alloy
        they employed,
bronze for arms and armour,
bronze for rooves: this was before
        the age of iron. They deployed

bare hands to wreak each other's
ruin which brought them
    to Hell's
dismal haunt, by now the nameless ones.
For all of their barbarity
    Death had dominion, its spells

forced them to leave the light   155
of day behind. And then in turn
    Earth took them over too
and Zeus created on good ground
another race — the fourth — both
    superior and more just, ones who

were godlike, a race of heroes,   160
in fact demigods. On this boundless
    earth they went before us.
The scourge of war obliterated
all of them. Some laid down lives
    fighting for the flocks of Oedipus

in Cadmus, outside the seven gates
of Thebes, while others still   165
    locked ships who'd sailed
across the main to Troy to win
the prize of fair-haired Helen
    and had not failed.

Death placed his pall across them
there, while others yet Zeus pitched
    at distant edges of the world,
away off on their own, and proffered
food and shelter. There
    they live on, enfurled   170

among the Islands of the Blest,
in sated harmony, along
    the shores of storm-tossed sea,
heroes happy in the certainty
their lands will yield a heap
    of grain that flows like honey,

and their three harvests every year.
Oh, would that I had died before
    or had not found my place
till afterward than been among the next,
the one that followed, fifth.
    This is the race

of iron. No rest in it. Day
and night, toil and tiredness
    take their grim
toll, their gift from gods a world
of cares, and theirs, whenever they are able,
    to take dim

with bright, the good with bad.
Zeus will exterminate them,
    those feeble ones, whose children
are born old and crowned with grey.
No more will offspring take
    after their fathers as when

once was the way, for now
when company comes calling (as in days
    gone by) friendship's flowers will be
found withered. Now no love's lost between
comrades and brothers, not as in those olden
    days. Sons and daughters are happy

175

180

185

to cut to the quick their quickly
ageing folk, the hard word
　　for them all, faulting, chiding
and chastising, and nare a care
about the gods' reprisals. They'll not
　　contribute to abiding

costs of keep — culprits all —
they'll plunder one another's towns.
　　But he, whose　　　　　　　　　　190
word's his bond, who cleaves
to law, won't be rewarded,
　　though they, those who lose

all sense of proper ways and commit wrongs
will be applauded when it's a fist's force
　　that determines what is right
and shame's not long gone out the door.
It's all hurt to the good from the worse
　　of the worst through the bleak night

of words that are lies, though sworn
to be true. It's working men
　　the Jealousy Plague will afflict,　　195
a green grim fury that feeds
on others' misery until Shame,
　　their nemesis, deems to constrict

their fair forms in faded mantles
and, forsaking man, makes
　　her way back to Mount
Olympus, leaving behind the ways
of this wide world to join　　　　　　200
　　the race of the immortals, the fount

of woes and sorrow now the lot
of man, left to the bite and bile
    of harm. And now,
for noblemen who'll understand
my meaning, I'll tell
    a tale, how

in the sky a hawk snatched
in his claws a speckle-
    necked nightingale, and she,
impinioned on his arced talons,
cried, 'Pity me'. But he dismissed
    her plaint and plea.

'There's little point in bawling.
Quit. You're in your master's grip.
    You'll go wherever
I direct, your night song notwithstanding.
Who knows? I might decide to gobble you
    or let you go. You think it clever

to pit your wit and strength against
your betters. You'll lose and learn,
    on top of your defeat, the shame
of loss.' So said the quickflying hawk,
flapping its far-reaching wings.
    Perses, your aim,

should be to restrain yourself
from reckless thought or deed,
    all injury to the indigent.
The good find burdens foist on them
that they don't want,
    first steps for those hellbent

on a fall. The way to decency's
a fairer one. Pit justice
    head to head
with egregious offence — stand back
and watch as it prevails. Learning's a heavy load
    only on a fool. Oaths are misled

alongside buckled ordinance.
Justice is dragged screaming   220
    from judges ravenous for bribes,
who bend the rules of law to their own
ends. In veils behind a shroud
    of fog she circumscribes

the homes of men bringing them
to rack and ruin, who distort
    her truths and would repel
her. But those who answer true,   225
keep faith with customary codes
    when citizens and aliens as well

present before the courts, will find
their home ground prosper
    and their townsfolk blossom.
Then youth-promoting Peace
permeates the motherland and Zeus,
    all seeing, releases them from

threats and throes of war.
Those who adhere to nature's laws   230
    are spared a fall. No
hunger brings them to their knees.
They'll have their fill at harvest homes.
    Earth will bestow

a rich reward. Their oakheads
swell with acorns. Their oakhearts
    swarm with honey bees.
Flocks sway beneath
235   their heavy fleeces and mothers
    produce progenies

the spit image of their fathers.
Such beneficence abounds
    and croplands lavish
affluence so there's no need
to risk the waves. Farsighted
    Zeus, Cronos' son, will wish

to condemn wanton ones, who scheme
240   vile acts. For often one man's
    machinations did grind
a city to the ground when he adopted
outlaw ways and set his mind on malice.
    Then from on high Zeus consigned

a pestilence, plague and famine
that wasted men past skin and bone.
    Whole families
in death's clasp, a barrenness on women,
245   through the wish of Zeus, his father's son,
    whose retribution shatters armies

and armadas, the very walls
of settlements. My lords, attend
    with care to the very thought
of this — that among mankind
gods go always, alert to those
250   who with poor judgement care naught

and spill scorn on the notion
of reprisals from above and wear
         their fellows down to finest
dust. Three times three thousand
guardians — more, in fact,
         immortal ones at Zeus' behest

while covered in their mist-
mantle, patrol the world, its network
         of provinces providing
for even more of them, and oversee   255
wrongs done and sentences
         betiding

them. And then there's Justice,
Zeus's very own daughter,
         a maiden with command
of gods' respect on Mount Olympus
and who, when she's abused with lies,
         sits at the right hand

of her father, Zeus, son of Cronos,
and regales him with reports   260
         of men's foul hearts
and minds, until the people pay
a price for leaders who pervert
         through devious acts and arts

her course of control. Obey
what she ordains, you who say
         you show the way, you
ministers of bribes and backhanders,
set the record straight. Cut out
         your crooked ways. He who

265 wrongs another wrongs himself
most of all. Foul plots rebound
upon the doer, the one who fails
himself. There's nothing Zeus can't see
or know — what's here, for instance,
and how the scales

of Justice balance in this place.
270 The way things are, let it be
neither me nor mine who predicts
the path of righteousness, for there's folly
in the rightful way when villainy
wins its rewards and verdicts

of the court. I hold still that Zeus
will not sanction such habitude.
Take this, Perses,
275 to heart and heed the prompt
of equity. Abjure
your violent ways.

Such Zeus laid down as law
for men though wild beasts
and creatures of the height
and depth of heaven are ignorant
of such decrees and feed
on one another. Right,

or rightness, the choice of qualities,
he bestowed to man.
280 Far-seeing Zeus, favour those
with blessings who preach
and practise it. But those who
wittingly and willingly chose

to lie, although sworn witnesses,
and in their recklessness
	trample fairness underfoot, their offsprings'
stock will thin and evanesce
while those whose word stands strong   285
	will smile at what fortune brings.

These themes are worth attending to;
you need to hear and heed them,
	Perses. Try,
you dunce. Wickedness will trap you
in any of its many ways — there's
	an easy level road to it, and it hardby.

But good is harder grasped,
for the immortal gods have placed
	all kinds of stumbling blocks 290
between us. That way's all
uphill and long, and rough
	at the beginning, with craggy rocks

until you reach the crest. There
the hardship falls away
	from finding it. The best of men
is one with his own mind,
who thinks ahead and weighs up
	what's in store. Or one who'll listen 295

to sound advice. But he,
that thoughtless one who will not
	learn from others' lessons, what's he
but a dead loss? You, Perses,
you who were well bred, attend.
	Keep what I say in mind and be

careful to ensure that hunger
is your enemy and Demeter,
300   revered and wreathed in garlands, the one
who smiles on you and piles your barns
with plenty, for hunger rests easily
  with a slothful man whom none

of gods or better men can bear —
he's but a drone, all buzz, no sting,
  and does naught but eat,
305 a profligate of bees' industry. So learn
to make a plan. Stick to a course
  to make your granary replete

with offerings of every season.
Through diligence and application
  men's flocks expand
and they amass a golden hoard,
as well as blessings of both
310   Infinites and the good who will not stand

for laziness. Don't be ashamed
of work. The shame lies in its opposite.
  Work — and you'll soon see
the lazybones turn green with envy;
lasting fame can be your just
  reward, and well earned bounty.

Whatever fortune comes your way
work enhances it. Don't be a fool,
315   with one eye fixed on other
men's possessions. Count
your blessings, pay your way.
  This is worth listening to, brother.

Shame that comes to nothing
escorts the poor, though shame,
    a blessing and a curse,
can prompt a man to ruin
or advantage. Humiliation
    introduces poverty — or worse —

while from fearlessness a betterment
ensues. Nothing filched or pilfered,   320
    prefer the gifts from gods.
If by the use of might a man
usurps a fortune or by his slick
    and silver tongue stacks odds

and such occurs when lusts
for selfish gains beguile
    a mind and belittle
fellow men in ruthlessness —
then gods will subjugate him   325
    and whittle

down his holdings. Wealth won
that way will topple in a trice.
    A whiff of wind could blow
away wealth unearthed like that.
Just as bad, abuse of those
    who plead and pray for aid you know

or don't, or sleeping with
your brother's wife, all your esteem
    doused in her chamber's dark
or if, through ignorance, you injure   330
orphans or hurl the bitter word
    towards a patriarch

perched on the doorstep
of declining years. Such offences
    and inequities incur
the ire of Zeus himself
on which he'll dole his dire sentence.
335   Put a snaffle on your

thoughts towards such ends.
Pay gods a tithe, one
    without a string attached. Hence
take the best of hams to honour them.
Try to please and to appease
    them with incense

and libations when sleep-time
falls and a heavenly light
    emerges from the sky at night.
340 They'll smile then on your interests
and your undertakings and you'll hold on to
    your holdings and might

even supplement them. Break
bread with friends, shun foes.
    Be mindful of the true
value of good neighbours. Should misfortune
brush against your house they'll rush
    to help, even if they do

345 appear in night attire, while family
and relations dally and dither
    getting dressed.
The bad neighbour is a bane,
the good a boon. Who lives beside
    a good neighbour is truly blessed.

With decency next door
you needn't worry about strays.
  Be fair in all
dealings with them. Return at least
as much as you receive
   and, if you've the wherewithal,   350

maybe more along with it.
That way there'll be enough
  when you've a want
on you. Ill gains precede a fall.
Steer clear of them. Reciprocate
   when you are loved. Be a font

of help when you're asked
for assistance. Accept donations —
  and repay them. Stint
on the mean. Let those who give   355
receive. Leave the rest with one arm
   no longer than the other by dint

of their decision. It's good to give,
a crime to steal, a grievous risk.
  Give with open eyes
and all your heart, even a great gift,
and you'll bask in the glow of it,
   its satisfactions like a prize.

Should a blaggard pilfer even
a mere trifle a fist of ill
  grabs his soul and freezes it   360
to the core. As a stalk
to stalks to build a stook,
  add little to little, bit by bit,

to make a lot. He who will not
staves off the appetite
        that dulls whatever glint is in
your eye. What you have
to hand's no cause for fret.
        Home's a haven.

Dangerous waters lie beyond.
To want and be without —
        that hurts the heart. To feed
off what you have is good. Think
on this. Go easy in the middle
        of a barrel. If you've a need

drink your fill just as you
broach it or approach the bottom.
        There's little gain in leaving lees.
Let pay you promise
to a friend be stipulated
        in advance, even if he's

family; agree and then
have it attested. The risk's the same
        in trust as in distrust. Again
be wary of a woman's wiles, one
who's all sweet talk, come hither
        and come on, flirting to gain

all you're good for. Believe
a woman the way you'd place your trust
        in any one that's out to fleece
you. An only son secures
his father's holdings, with interest
        growing piece by piece

within the walls. If there's another
that man will have to live
        a longer life to restore
his assets. Zeus knows, however,
how a larger family prospers:
        more hands, more mouths, but more   380

help too — and greater gain.
If in your heart of hearts you can't
        but dream about luxuriance
here's what you have to do —
work and work. Add work to work
        when they begin their sprightly dance,

Atlas' daughters, seven sisters,
then start to reap,
        and when they slow
start to plow. For forty nights   385
and forty days they stay under-
        cover, out of sight, below,

but as the circle of the year
begins to rotate on its axis
        you'll see them as you edge
your sickle blades. Nature assigned
this law for every man,
        be his life on the ledge

of plains or by the shore,
or be it far inland he farms
        on hillside clearances. Sow on days   390
you'd strip to the waist; plow
and reap the same if you'd draw
        home the harvest in the ways

of its appointed season. Then
everything will thrive in time
        and need not force
you to knock on neighbours' doors
with the poor mouth. That's how,
        Perses, you enter discourse

with me, and I've offered now
as much as I am willing
        and you deserve. Work, you dope,
work. It's work the gods decreed for each
and everyone. You'll have
        the heavy heart as wife and young slope

off and slink in tow as you drag
yourself from door to door
        and find ears deaf to your petitions.
Oh yes, you'll find some kindness here
and some luck there, but bother
        them again and your submissions

of appeal will be a waste
of breath, and no avail.
        Your silver tongue will tarnish,
a useless instrument. Find a way
to pay back what you owe —
        and spare yourself the varnish

of the added hurt that's hunger.
First, build your house. Then
        source an ox to pull your plow
and fix a woman's price — no,
not the one to wed —
        to drive your team in this now

and in that then to keep
all things shipshape at home.
  So if a time should come when
you're at loss and have to ask
and be turned down
  you'll not be left heartbroken.

Don't postpone until tomorrow   410
or the day beyond what you
  could do today. Procrastination
never crammed a granary, nor the efforts
of a layabout. Good management
  ensures full approbation.

He who defers stares ruin
in the face. When the furnace
  of the sun is damped
by Zeus's autumn showers   415
a weight will slither from your shoulders
  and you'll find a lightness lamped

into you, for Sirius, the Dog Star
at Orion's heels, hangs over heads
  of mortal men a shorter time
and sleeps with night so sun
won't scorch the day. Fell trees   420
  whose shoots no longer climb

in spurts, their leafage shed,
then split them into blocks. You'll find
  they have the soundest wood. Pay heed.
Pay heed. It's high time now
for working in the forests.
  A yard-long log you'll need

to make your mortar, and half
as long again to make its pestle,
         a seven foot to make a gudgeon
425   though eight-foot lengths leave
more than enough to make a maul
         or mattock to bludgeon

clods. Use shorter cuts, offcuts,
455   to shape and fit the felloes
         in proportion to the flatbed of the cart.
You'll need bent bits for this.
Bear home a beam of oak — holm oak,
         to be precise — to make the 'tree' part

when you've searched both high and low
430   for it. This will stand best
         the test of ways your oxen plow
when your plowwright,
Athena's helper, first drills
         the share and now

drives home the dowels to fasten it.
Take care to keep two plows
         to hand, one which
is of a single piece, the other
joined and jointed. That's ideal —
         so if one breaks you hitch

435   the other to the team. Limbs
of elm and laurel resist woodworm.
         Preferred are plow-stocks
made of common oak, with beams
of holm. Keep a pair
         of nine-year-olds, ox

bulls in the full of health.
They'll stay strong, and last longer
  at the labour. They'll not toss
turned earth and won't kick out
nor smash the plow and leave   440
  the job abandoned. Let the boss

behind your team be no less
than the age of forty. A single loaf, four
  quarters or eight slices, he'll do
the work of two and follow
a straight furrow. Past the age
  of looking round to see who

might be there and everywhere,
he'll keep his eye on work   445
  to do. You'll not find
younger hands who'll broadcast
better or waste less seed.
  They're too inclined

on the social swirl. The crane,
home-bound on its yearly round,
  cries from a cloud
above her song, the prompt
that winter's here and wintry rains   450
  and time to say you've plowed

some land already. That call cuts
to the quick men with
  no oxen of their own.
It's time to have your big-horned
beasts brought on at home
  to prime condition, perfect muscle tone.

Easy then to say, 'Lead out
the team and waggon' and easier far
        to let a neighbour down
with your 'My oxen have their own
labours cut out in front of them.'
        That man's a clown

who thinks his waggon's all
but built, his fortune only
        in his head. Before he starts
he'll need a hundred lengths
of timber. Take time and trouble
        then to round up all the parts.

Come plowing time, make haste
to turn, you and your hands,
        towards work to be done, hail,
rain or shine. An early start
ensures abundance. The early
        start — you know the tale . . .

You can, of course, plow
early in the year. But land you've let
        lie fallow and turn in spring,
this will yield abundantly. Sow
that land while the soil's still light.
        That will spare some cursing

and be a future comfort.
Offer orisons to Zeus underground
        and Holy Demeter
to help her tickle the blessed seed
so that it laughs
        out loud. Offer

prayers the minute your hand
touches the handle of the plow
    and crack your whip across
the oxen's backs, as they apply
their shoulders to the yokes.
    Show who's boss.

Have a young lad follow with a hoe   470
unsettling birds that scrabble
    in the rows for broadcast
seed. For humankind
a house in order is nonesuch;
    the opposite the last

word in competitions for the worst.
With one the ears of corn will weigh
    the stacks towards the ground,
if Zeus himself gives
his consent. So dust   475
    the cobwebs from around

the storage jars and truly, truly,
truly you'll sing in jubilation
    when you begin with drawing
up what you've amassed
and barnfuls carry you
    as far as lightening spring

without the hungry eye
on the reserves of neighbours.
    They'll have to call on you by right.
But open ground upon the shortest
day and you'll reap wisps   480
    of sheaves and be a sorry sight

on hunkers in the dust as you strain
to make a stook of them. Who could
        look up to you if all that you can
carry home fits in a creel?
Zeus, who bears a goatskin shield,
        has a plan

for every man and moment,
a notion mortals struggle with.
485   They may, however, soon cavort,
those who start their plowing
late. When each cuckoo
        conjures its exact retort

out of oak groves and lifts
up hearts around the world
        rain follows
some days afterwards, courtesy again
of Zeus, but just as much
        as fills the hollows

490 of a bullock's hoof. This lets late
starters catch the early plower.
        Mind this
within your breast and take
a note of spring's appearance
        with its benefice

of blossoms and rain's arrival
when it's due. Keep walking past
        the forge and that mob
that dawdles at the door
on bitter days on which men shy
        from any job

that should be done. Keep your head   495
down at work and you'll add to
        your increase — and not feel
the force of winter want
and have to rub your wizened hand
        across the weals and blisters on each heel.

The indolent invests his faith
in hollow hopes. He's left with
        nothing. He turns the matter
of his need to wicked ways.
Empty dreams tempt those without   500
        and fill their lack with idle chatter.

Before midsummer's peak tell those
who work for you, 'Start a store and shelter.
        Would that summer were
more than a season!' Beware
the winter months whose winds
        would whip skin off an ox. Beware   505

those frosts that fix on earth their tight fist
when from the north
        squalls race and rumple seas
and roar through Thrace — home of
and hospitality to horses — while tilled lands
        and woodlands scream their agonies.

In wooded uplands there's a wind
that bashes hordes of high-crowned oaks
        and hardy firs and sweeps   510
them down to meet rich loam
as the whole range and reach
        of plantings roar heaps

of sufferings. Their tails between their legs,
creatures cower, creatures of the wild
    cry out their frighted note.
The lazy wind goes through
instead of round the pelts of brutes
    which wear a winter coat,

515   through their hides too, right
through them and bucks' thick fur.
    Only sheep don't feel,
wrapped in their shaggy fleeces,
the bite of Boreas, that north wind.
    It shapes an old man like a wheel

and bends him to its will,
but spares a maiden's gentle skin,
520   for she's at home, indoors,
with mother, as yet untouched
by Aphrodite's lovesome charms;
    she bathes her tender pores

and smoothes and soothes them
with lavender before she settles
    in the refuge of her room.
That's how it is in winter
when One-with-no-bone
525   gnaws his own foot in the gloom

of derny dens that he inhabits,
hearthless places, without a way to find
    his feeding grounds, for no sun casts spell
enough; no, it scarcely brightens all of Greece
but hangs over the heads of those
    who live where black men dwell.

Then the denizens of woods, horned
and hummel, break through the brush,
    their teeth a-chatter from the shock 530
of cold, their hearts set on a single
goal, past the windbreak
    of a chambered rock.

Then men advance, their sticks
and staves the spit of a third leg,
    bent over double,
their foreheads grope the ground
as they move to outwit tumbling snow. 535
    Then spare no trouble

to wrap up well, and wear
a well tanned tunic and homespun cloak.
    On slight or slender warp weave
hefty threads for warmth, and those
hairs standing on your neck
    you'll relieve,

and your body, wracked with shivers, 540
won't be perished with the cold.
    Shape sandals from the raw-
hide of a slaughtered ox, line them
with a shearling's wool or rabbit fur
    and draw

them tightly to your ankles.
Come bitterest cold, sew skins
    of yearling kids with leather
thongs and bundle up in them
to keep hailstones at bay. Wear 545
    a woollen hat against the weather

and keep your ears comfortable
and cosy. There's nothing like the cold
          of mornings when the north wind
blows and clammy fogs slump
from starry skies to lie like blankets
          swaddling all your disciplined

550   endeavours in the wheat fields. There's
a certain mist that emanates
          from constant rivers,
that tempests raise to cloud the earth —
sometimes it comes at night as rain,
          other times as shivers

of wind when Thracian gales
bustle, gust and blast. Race
          this wind — turn a blind eye
555   to work and hurry home, checking that
that sombrous cloud won't shed its load on you
          and soak you to the marrow. Don't shy

from winter weather and storms
that go with it to make this a month
          that's hard on men and hard
on flocks. Cut back on cattle feed.
Give more to men than usual
560   because the road to morning's marred

by its length. Mind this until
year's end when Mother Earth presents
          her opulence, pitching days that jar
against the hours of nights until — by grace
of Zeus — you've counted sixty days
565   from winter solstice and the star

Arcturus rises from the holy
waters of Oceanus, a new blaze
    at evening time, and the swallow,
mournful daughter of Pandion,
wails her way into the sky to herald
    spring. Best to follow   570

this by trimming vines. Then,
when He-who-bears-his-house-
    upon-his-back slowly scales
the plants, stealing away from Pleiades,
quit hoeing weeds to edge your sickles —
    and make a sound that hails

the help. Don't dally in the shade
nor sleep past dawn when the crop
    is ripe to reap and sun-
scorch a present threat. Get up   575
before the crack of dawn and bring
    the harvest home, your one

and only store and good supply. Dawn.
Dawn accounts for one whole
    third of your chores. Dawn sets
you up for jobs and journeys.
Its coming fixes yokes to many's
    the ox and gets   580

men on the go. When thistle's
in full fluff and from their perches
    in the melting pot
of summer cicadas ratchet their shrill
racket and goats are at their   585
    fattest, grapes at their prime, there's not

an end to women's wanting, though men
are at their weakest worst,
     worn out by Sirius, in mind and limb,
and the weather shrivelling
their skin. What better then
     than a sheltered nook, and for him

a cake of bread baked recently
and washed down with the finest wine
     and the last of goat's cheese
from the height of August and a meal
of meat from free-range maiden
     heifers, as yet unmated kids. At ease,

with deep goblets of gleaming red
you sit in shade, replete,
     before refreshing breezes riffling west
from mountain peaks. Mix three parts
water, from a free-flowing
     rivulet, and one part of the best

vintage; then, when sword-armed Orion
straddles the horizon, exhort the men
     to flail the holy grain of Demeter
in well aired threshing rings. Weigh
it first — then lay it up in hoppers.
     What better

then, when you've your harvest safe
and sound and under cover, to take on
     a hired hand, simply bred,
and a woman who's no children yet —
for a nursing woman is a burden.
     Keep a long-fanged hound well fed

590

595

600

and wary of He-who-walks-at night,
the Day Sleeper who'd burgle you.
        Ensure that there's a fill
of fodder and clean bedding
for the mules and oxen. That done,
        grant weary workers a moment to be still

when they've unharnessed and un-
hooked their teams. Let them
        relax and find repose.
When the Hunter and Dogstar achieve
the apex of the south and Dawn,
        Dawn with its rose-   610

fingers, surmounts Arcturus, time then,
Perses, to gather grapes and cart them home.
        Expose them to the sun
for all of ten days and as many nights.
Then store them in a shade for five
        before what must be done,

next day, the sixth, transporting
to your vats Dionysus' benefice.
        But when they set,
Pleiades and Hyades and brave Orion,   615
it's time to turn the earth again for it
        to bear next year's supply. Don't you forget

this ever. But if an urge
comes over you to sail
        the ruffled waves, when the Pleiades
outrun Orion's wrath and dive   620
into churned depths and there are offshore
        turmoils, storms and furies,

forsake the sea, that wine-
dark realm, and accept this advice —
    stick to the labours of the land.
Haul your ship ashore and moor
625   it fast by lashing it with rocks
    and stones that will withstand

the best the winds can blow. Unplug
a bung so sitting rain won't rot
    the bilge. Stow your gear
neatly in your house when carefully
you've rolled up your sails. They're what
    will help a vessel sheer

across the water. Hang up your rudder
by your smoky hearth and wait,
630   wait for that time to show
for you to set out on the seaway.
When that hour comes launch
    your speeding ship and pack its cargo

tightly so you'll come home a winner.
This, Perses, you dolt, is how
    our father fared, propelled by appetite
to improve his lot. Once he set sail
635   from the home place in Aeolian Cyme
    and after a rough crossing set sight

on here and landed. He wasn't
on the run from wealth untold,
    the easy life, no, not at all,
but fleeing from the ways of want
Zeus deals to men sometimes. Near Helicon
    he built a home, a place that some call

Ascra, a backward place, in summer
bad, in winter worse, at any time   640
          indeed a dead end and dead
loss. Remember, brother, to everything
its time and season — and none
          more so than sailing. Set thoughts ahead

on little ships, but load your freight
in larger ones. The more you take
          on board the more you stand to make.
Work on top of work earns its reward
if you're spared savage storms at sea.   645
          If, and when, you try to stake

your half-wit in the trade to get
off the hook of debt and hungers
          eating at you I'll dispense
instructions in the ways that govern
waves (though I couldn't call
          myself in any sense

an authority on ships or sailing),
I, who never have embarked   650
          on sea, by which I mean
the 'open' sea, unless you count
the ferry from Aulis to Euboea
          when once a host of Achean

seamen survived a gale to cross
from sacred Greece to Troy, the land
          of lovely women. From there I navigated
to Chalkis for ceremonies planned to honour   655
Amphidamas and the conferring
          of awards his big-hearted sons inaugurated.

That's where I triumphed in the singing
competition and earned a trophy I dedicated
    to the Muses of Mount Helicon
who made me a master in the art
of song. Though that's my sum of knowledge
    about well put-together vessels I can go on

660   and speak for Zeus, Zeus with
the goat-skinned shield, for the Muses
    taught me more than how to sing.
They bestowed on me the matter
and the makings of a song. For fifty days,
    leaving the longest day behind, leaving

     the worst of summer's drudge,
665   sailing's safe, there'll be no
    wrecks, no loss of life at sea,
barring Poseidon's will, that is,
Poseidon the earth shatterer, or Zeus,
    first of the firsts, decides by his decree

an end of you. These two,
between them, these dictate
    the best and worst laid out
670   for us. Breezes then blow straight
and true, and there's no harm
    abroad the deep. So flout

convention and your cautions, keep faith,
and launch your rapid craft
    and load it to the gunwales.
Hurry homeward soon as you are able —
well before vendanges and autumn's starts
    of rain, winning the race with winter when all's

a spurting wind on its way north.
These winds succeed torrential showers
 Zeus dispatches and ruffle white locks
of the waves so that sea passage is
a chore. There's a second chance
 for setting out to sea, when there rocks

on a fig tree's tippy top in spring
a leaf that's no bigger than
 the claw marks of a crow —
then the way's open again. The way
and season for seafaring.
 Not that I know

a single word to say for it — there's
no heartlift in it for me.
 A simple twist of fate — and ruin
stares you in the face. But that
holds no one back. There's no such thing
 as common sense. What to do in

such circumstances no man thinks clearly,
half-wit that he is: money means
 the world to him. Death in deep folds
of water is a grim demise
so I repeat, heed my advice.
 Don't hazard all you own in the holds

of ships. Leave more ashore
than you stack up on board.
 All you risk at sea's
a living dread — as woeful as the outcome
of an overloaded waggon, an axle
 split in two fair halves, a tragedy's

unravelling before your very eyes.
Know your limits; allow fair time
                for all you undertake. Give or take,
695   in your late twenties present
        a woman as your wife. Time then
                to tie the knot. She'd make

        the best to marry, a woman in her
        teens, a virgin bride, a willingness
700   to learn. Select someone
        from the neighbourhood, one you know
        all about so she'll not make
                a laughing stock of you. There's none

        or nothing better for a man than a good
        wife, nothing worse than this
                mistake — a sow that in the stall
        hogs the trough, one who'll eat
        him out of house and home and gives
                her man, strong and all

        as he may be, a thorough roasting,
705   though there be no fire. She'll put
                years on him before his time.
        Fear retribution from the gods above,
        the eternal ones. Don't let
                the way you treat a friend chime

        with the way you treat a brother.
        Or, if you do, don't throw
                the first stone in a row —
        nor wag a loose tongue for the sake
710   of saying something. And if a friend
                affronts you by how

he speaks or what he does
pay him back in duplicate. But if he
        extends an olive branch, elect
to accept it. There is no honour
in switching social circles. Let
        your countenance reflect

your disposition. Don't open doors   715
either to too many or to none.
        Don't quarrel with greathearts
or deal with scamps and scallywags. Don't mock
the pestilence of poverty that wears away
        the souls of men. It too starts

among the gods. The good word
is the jewel in your crown, no better   720
        joy than flows from it when
it's used well. The mean word floated
on the wind rebounds with double force.
        Be one of nature's gentlemen

at parties at which all those who
congregate divide the burden of expense
        and make of it a great
delight and little load. At matins never
raise your glass to Zeus or any other
        god before you expurgate   725

your hands. They'll stay deaf
to your entreaties — and hurl them
        back at you. Don't urinate upright
in plain daylight, but rather
in between the start and end of dark.
        Then don't go unclothed: night

is reserved for the divines. Don't
relieve yourself on or beside
    the byeway. Good etiquette
dictates you hunker in the shade
of a sheltered stead. At home
    don't huddle by the hearth, nor let

your private parts be in plain view
for all to see, agleam with sweat
    and glaze after you've come.
735 Stay clear of this. Father your young
on your return from some ambrosial
    banquet, not from some

ill-fated funeral. Always, before
you ford fair flowing streams,
    be careful to complete
ablutions with the cleanest water
and first utter a prayer, your eyes affixed
    to their surface. That man whose feet

740 enter a river with maculate mind
and hands unhallowed gods bear
    ill-will; he'll pay the price before
too long. And don't ever, in heat
of festive moments, pare the deadnail
    from the quick of your

five-fingered limb. Nor ever let
them, as they drink, leave a ladle
745   balanced above the mixing bowl —
there's risk of ruination here. Add
to your home and house a final touch,
    some auspicious emblem or aureole,

so no crow will perch on it
to croak and caw. When you dine
    or wash use neither bowl nor
basins you've not consecrated:
hurt or harm is sure to follow.
    Be they but twelve days old or   750

twelve years, there's little good
in boys, sitting in sacred places.
    That steals the marrow from the bone
when they grow up. Nor should a man
anoint himself with water from
    a woman's bath — he'll pay unknown

costs some day. Or if he happens on   755
a sacrificial fire let him not mock
    something beyond his understanding.
Somewhere there's a god he'll vex.
Don't foul the waters of an estuary
    or well — don't go landing

yourself in trouble for insulting
water gods. These aren't the places
    to find yourself in debt
to need. Pay heed to me — and don't forget   760
the damage idle gossip does. A bad
    name's as easily got as a wet

foot and harder to recover from.
You know how flung dung sticks.
    What's said about you clings
if it's in the mouths of many. It has
a power like a god's. Days are a gift   765
    from Zeus; be one who sings

their due, indicating to the labour
force the thirtieth of every month
      as choice for checking on the work
and doling out provisions. These are
the days that he despatches, Zeus
      himself, all wise. Don't shirk —

770   if you would know yourself and choose
to do the best you can. First among
      the holy days are, yes,
the first, the fourth, the seventh.
That seventh's when Apollo of the golden
      sword was born to Leto. Stress

too the eighth and ninth from moon's
beginning as best for taking on
      a task. The eleventh and, some say,
775   the twelfth are next as good for clipping
sheep or drawing home a harvest.
      The twelfth is even better than the day

before, if truth be told. Spiders
waver in mid-air and spin
      their lifelines. And that wise one, the ant,
when this day's at its height, stacks
his stores high. For a woman to kickstart
      her loom and set to weave it can't

780   be bettered. Don't begin to broadcast
seed on the thirteenth day from
      month's beginning, tend
then to plants by landing them. The sixth
day of the middle quarter
      is no good day to spend

on them. But it's one that's
auspicious for the births of boys.
      Not so for girls — and no luck
for their wedding days. It's true, the sixth day 785
of the month's first moiety bodes poorly
      for the births of girls, but squeezing buck

kids and ram lambs is good. And pens assembled
and erected for the flocks fare well. More chance
      on this day of boys being born
who'll cut you with their tongues,
who'll lie and wheedle you, conducting
      talk in nods and winks and scorn.

And on the eighth day cut your boar 790
and roaring bull and toss away
      the stones. And on the twelfth likewise
geld your mules. But men
born on the twentieth, at the apex
      of that great day, are wise

and are good mediators. Their minds
work overtime. The tenth is also
      good for births of boys, the fourth, mid-
month, is good for girls. This is 795
the day to handle ewes and ambling
      beasts with straggly horns, to bid

your white-fanged hounds and donkeys
made for work be quieter, as pets.
      And don't forget the risk
attaching to the fourth day of the moon
as it wanes and waxes, for it could be
      the death of you! Be brisk

in bringing home a bride on any month's
first fourth day, first having read
  the best omens of birds. Beware
the fifth — *every* fifth — that's the day
will break your heart. It was the fifth,
  they say, the Furies were

midwives when Oath was born,
whom Strife bore to make life
  difficult for those who'd lie.
Before pouring out the sacred grain
of Demeter on the perfect circle of a well-
  tamped threshing floor, cast a cautious eye

on the month's second seventh. This, truly,
is the day for sawyers to splice
  beams for a home-building, and plenty
of neat-fitting planks for ships. Begin
on the fourth constructing your sleek boats.
  On the month's second ninth, you'll see

improvements towards evening,
though men are safest on the first.
  That first ninth's a goodly day
to beget and to be born. A good day
indeed. Not many know the twenty-
  seventh's choice to broach a barrel, say,

to yoke matched pairs of mules
and oxen, to fit smart-stepping horses
  to a chariot, or to haul
down to the wine-dark sea a ship
equipped for many rowers.
  Not many call

this by its proper name. Break out
the wine when it's the fifth. The month's
        second fourth is a holy day always.
Likewise not many know the day
after the twentieth glows at dawning
        but fares less well towards day's

end. To men on earth such days
are godsends. The others matter less.
        They're changeable. No Fate
has singled them. There's no one who has not
pet days, but who knows anything
        for sure? Some days make us feel separate,

others proffer mother's love. For he
is truly blessed and he has all
        the luck who learns the song
of deeds and their days and holds his head
up high before the gods, who reads and heeds
        the signs of birds and steers clear of any wrong.

820

825

Afterwords

Hail to thee, Italy, holy mother of all that grows,
mother of men — in your honour I plunged into material
and measures
prized in days of old, daring to divulge its hallowed sources
and sing a hymn to work and days through the towns of Rome.
       — *The Georgics of Virgil*, Book Two, 173-176

When I published in 2004 a translation of *The Georgics*, parts
of which poem first cast a spell on me when, at the age of nine,
I started learning Latin at St Gerard's School, I was surprised
by a question several people put to me: 'What are you going
to translate next?' My instinctive, immediate response was,
'Nothing.' I didn't think of myself as a translator.

I know, of course, there are admirable poets who turn
from one text to another. I think at once of David Ferry who,
alongside his academic career and his own poems, has completed versions of the epic *Gilgamesh,* the *Odes of Horace*
and the *Eclogues of Virgil*. His translation of the *Georgics*
appeared in 2005, the year after mine. In his tenth decade he
finished a new *Aeneid*.

A closer friend, Seamus Heaney, in his interest in and
exploration of the whole canon of world literature, published
divers translations of Irish poetry, most notably the Middle
Irish *Buile Suibhne (Sweeney Astray)* and Brian Merriman's
Cúirt an Mheán Oíche (The Midnight Verdict), some cantos
of Dante, *The Testament of Cresseid and Seven Fables* from
the Scots of Robert Henryson, excerpts and poems by Ovid
and Pascoli and two dramatic versions of Sophocles, *The
Cure at Troy* and *The Burial at Thebes.* If the effort involved
in making a *Beowulf* for our time was, as he said, akin to hard
labour his engagement with Book VI of the *Aeneid* reads like
the work of a man on parole.

Soon after I published *The Georgics* I included in *The
Company of Horses* adaptations of passages from Ovid and I
had completed a draft of Hesiod's poem commonly rendered

as *Works and Days* with that freedom that follows a response such as my 'Nothing'. I felt I'd cleared the way to pursue the essence of the Greek that had provided a model for Virgil's 'poem of the earth'. In the age of the creation of a literature to match the founding of a Roman empire poets in Latin looked to Greek antecedents for models. For Virgil's pastoral suite, the *Eclogues*, there was the *Idylls* of Theocritus. For the *Aeneid,* an epic poem which begins at sea, there was Homer. For the *Georgics* there was Hesiod's version of man's origins, ancient almanac and instructions for the best way to conduct a life, *Works and Days*. I needed to investigate what Virgil found in it and took from it.

The very opening lines of Virgil's poem, with their appeal to his patron, Mycaenas, shadowed the opening invocations of Hesiod's, first to the Muses to proclaim praise to Zeus, then to Zeus himself, a plea. Both poems present a set of moral cases. Both say, Who wrongs another wrongs himself most of all. Both advocate that work leads to bounty and fame. Hesiod's description of the slothful man as 'a drone, all buzz, no sting . . . a profligate of bees' industry' (c.301-305) strikes a note Virgil elaborates in his emblem of a hive as the ideal of human cooperation and social intercourse. Virgil's 'Plow on days you'd strip to the waist; sow the same' (Book One, 299) repeats the instructions of Hesiod's line 390 'Sow on days/you'd strip to the waist; plow and reap the same . . . '

By ascribing particular dates of the month to certain deeds and actions Virgil in 1.277 replicates Hesiod's matter and manner — 'Beware the fifth . . . ', in 1.284 'The seventeenth's a lucky day . . . ' and in 1.286 'The ninth day smiles on any-one who runs away, but frowns on those who steal,' with no more reason given for the 'truth' of his catalogue of claims than the earlier writer. Were they a wisdom born of folk custom or sets of superstition or, might we dare to hope, the fruit of record or of attentions paid? While Hesiod writes of the Islands of the Blest with their 'three harvests every year' (c.174) Virgil has 'Twice cattle calve each year and twice the apple trees present their plenty' (2.150). Hesiod describes a golden age for man

> *. . . theirs was good life,*
> *   peace and plenty and the best*

> *of flocks* (c.120)

while Virgil proclaims

> *If they but knew! They're steeped in luck, country people,*
> *being far removed from grinds of war, where earth that's*
> *   just*
> *showers them with all they could ever ask for.* (2.458-460)

However much we learn that Virgil steals from Hesiod his
poem is not in any way diminished. Its absolute coherence
and opulence of thought and image protect its special majesty.
Both poets urge the veneration of gods and payment of yearly
offerings but Virgil's conditions are social, national, Hesiod's
more personal. To read their poems together is a lesson in the
nature and usefulness of tradition.

Virgil is a most reticent poet about himself. He tells little
about his own life. Not so Hesiod. Or, at least, the speaker of
the poem Hesiod composed. We're told that the brother,
Perses, was 'well bred', that their father was

> *   propelled by appetite*
> *to improve his lot. Once he set sail*
> *from the home place in Aeolian Cyme*
> *   and after a rough crossing set sight*

> *on here and landed. He wasn't*
> *on the run from wealth untold,*
> *   the easy life, no, not at all,*
> *but fleeing from the ways of want*
> *Zeus deals to men sometimes. Near Helicon*
> *   he built a home, a place that some call*

Ascra, a backward place, in summer
bad, in winter worse, at any time
> *indeed a dead end and dead*
loss . . . (c.635-640)

He admits to knowing little about seafaring, though once
he sailed from Aulis to Chalkis in Euboea to participate in
funeral games for Amphidamas at which he won a prize — a
tripod — he

> *dedicated*
> *to the Muses of Mount Helicon*
> *who made me a master in the art*
> *of song.* (c.658)

If the drama of the poem's beginning lies in Hesiod's con-
stant berating of Perses who, when their inheritance was
being divided, 'snatched/the bigger half', the mode of
address is also striking. The speaker tells his brother things
he'd likely know already and is in fact consciously commu-
nicating with a wider audience. The advantages of industry
over indolence are sounded in the opening lines and returned
to frequently. Indeed, Perses' fate for his usurpation is
echoed in the prices to be exacted for other acts of betrayal
— the theft by Prometheus of fire, the creation of Pandora
and the grievous griefs that fell to man following the release
of her container's contents. His recurring theme is the pro-
motion of fair dealing — good fortune lies in store for honest
ones — and his advice is laced with warning: 'Ill gains precede
a fall.' (c.352) The adherence he promotes to nature's laws
for benefits and rewards would clearly mesh with Virgil's
notions of good husbandry. Like Virgil, the speaker of Hesiod's
poem would have the members of his community, as John
Cheever wrote of John Updike's characters, 'perform their
lives amid a landscape — a moral and a spiritual one — of
whose grandeur they were unaware.'

By the time I reached the end of my first version in 2006 I knew it lacked something. Soon afterwards I wondered if that was all my fault. I began to suspect different tones in the original and to question whether it was all the work of the same author. I had no expertise to check the Greek for fault lines or patches. I turned my back on Hesiod but he wouldn't go away. I attempted three subsequent versions, the main uses of which were to copper-fasten my interest in the poem and to enhance my sense of its merit, however flawed it was. I persisted with what must be the translator's aim and aspiration: to honour the original. In the autumn of 2015 I recast it completely. By discovering and affixing rhymes I shaped a stanza that might allow it to be read as I thought it should be, that is, quickly, with the rhymes as stepping stones in an extended game of hopscotch.

I appreciate that there is something spurious about the idea of a 'translation' or a 'version' of a poem by one who doesn't know the language of the original. But there are celebrated and successful precedents. See Ezra Pound. For Robert Lowell they were 'Imitations', for Derek Mahon, though he has several of the languages, they are 'Adaptations'. James Dickey, with a typical insouciance, called them 'Re-writes'. More recently, in *Memorial*, the English poet Alice Oswald writes, 'This is a translation of the *Iliad*'s atmosphere, not its story ... I write through the Greek, not from it — aiming for translucence rather than translation.'

By following a course through Virgil via ten or a dozen different versions in English of Hesiod's poem, I kept as a touchstone an idea in a passage by the Irish-language poet Máirtín Ó Direáin (1910-88). In 'Faoistiní' ('Confessions') from *Ó Mórna agus Dánta Eile* (*Ó Mórna and Other Poems*, 1957) he writes of the people of his native Inishmore in the Aran Islands being absolved by a priest:

Sciúradh is glanadh
Le slis na haithrí
Is briathra Laidne;

Briathra nár thuig
Ach gur thuigeadar astu.

(They were scoured and cleansed
By a sliver of repentance
And the words in Latin;
Words they didn't understand
But which they understood out of.)

So, if I was drawn to Hesiod because of what his work meant to Virgil, what it stood for for him, its place in his thinking and development, and how it influenced him, what might be the appeal of his poem now? It is a poem which pioneers the personal voice. It offers insights into social classes and customs in ancient times. Above all, perhaps, it is valuable for its advocacy of human virtues and for its articulation of eternal verities in one of their earliest iterations.

Loughcrew,
August 2017

Acknowledgements

Excerpts from *Deeds and their Days,* in different form, appeared in *Landmarks* (Poetry Now International Festival 2010) and *Twelve by Two for Terence* (School of English, Trinity College Dublin, 2010).

Sojourns in Ballynahinch and at the Tyrone Guthrie Centre at Annaghmakerrig helped in the making of this rendition. To Ed Downe for the former and the staff, Director and Board for the latter, I give thanks.

Acknowledgements are due to Jean Fallon, Aifric Mac Aodha, John McAuliffe and, especially, Andrew McNeillie for their careful readings of drafts of this work and encouragement towards its publication. I am grateful, too, to Anne Duggan and Suella Holland for their good work and camaraderie at The Gallery Press.

Hesiod: Homeric Hymns, Epic Cycle, Homerica translated by Hugh G Evelyn White (Harvard University Press, Loeb Classical Library, 1914)

Hesiod: The Works and Days, Theogony, The Shield of Herakles translated by Richmond Lattimore (The University of Michigan Press, 1959)

Hesiod: Theogony, Works and Days translated by Dorothea Wender (Penguin Books, 1973)

Hesiod: Theogony and Works and Days translated by M L West (Oxford University Press, 1988)

Hesiod: Theogony, Works and Days, Shield translated by Apostolos N Athanassakis (The Johns Hopkins University Press, 1983)

Hesiod: Works and Days and Theogony translated by Stanley Lombardo (Hackett Publishing Company, 1993)

Hesiod: Works and Days translated by David W Tandy and Walter C Neale (University of California Press, 1996)

Works of Hesiod and the Homeric Hymns translated by Daryl Hine (The University of Chicago Press, 2005)

Hesiod: Theogony and Works and Days translated by Catherine M Schlegel and Henry Weinfield (The University of Michigan Press, 2006)

Hesiod: Theogony, Works and Days, Testimonia translated by Glenn W Most (Harvard University Press, Loeb Classical Library, 2006)